Portrait of
TAUNTON
THE TOWN & THE VALE

Portrait of
TAUNTON
THE TOWN & THE VALE

GEOFF ROBERTS

Introduction by Robert Dunning

Captions by Andrew Hopkins, Kathy Epps and Robert Dunning

Somerset Books

First published in 2000 by Somerset Books
Image copyright © 2000 Geoff Roberts

ISBN 0 86183 416 X

British Library Cataloguing-in-Publication-Data
A CIP data record for this book is available from the British Library

SOMERSET BOOKS
Official Publisher to Somerset County Council

Halsgrove House
Lower Moor Way
Tiverton EX16 6SS
T: 01884 243242
F: 01884 243325
www.halsgrove.com

Printed and bound in Italy
by Centro Grafico Ambrosiano, Milan

*Readers are reminded that many of the properties featured in this book are not
open to the public, and are advised to consult the Taunton Tourist Information Centre
for details of any opening before attempting to gain admission.*

CONTENTS

Introduction   7

IN THE TOWN   9

OUT AND ABOUT   69

INTRODUCTION

A faire and pleasant towne this is I assure you. So wrote Thomas Gerard of Trent in the 1630s about Taunton; and he went on to mention its market, its manufactures, its buildings and its surrounding gardens and orchards. He had much less to say about Wellington, Wiveliscombe and Milverton; only that they were, respectively, 'good', 'slender' and 'ordinary' market towns.

A rather staccato gazetteer produced in the 1930s by the Royal Automobile Club declared Milverton a 'shrunken one-time market-town', Wiveliscombe an 'old agricultural town in lap of picturesque hills', Wellington a 'pleasant little market and educational town' and Taunton 'historic… delightfully situated in fertile Vale of Taunton Deane and forming extremely attractive motoring centre'.

Motorists travelling to the South West in the 1960s had a different view of both Taunton and Wellington, nose-to-tail in traffic queues. Now a motorway takes the through traffic and summer Saturdays are no more busy than any other Saturday. But they are quite busy enough, and Taunton's weekday rush-hours, morning and evening, bring cries for an inner bypass and an end to the inconvenience of a level crossing over a busy railway.

Taunton and its neighbours, like most places, should be seen on foot and not through the windows of a car; and seen at leisure. Only then, and with the help of images in this book – to be used as guides before and aides memoires after – will the various layers of history become apparent. Much is successfully hidden, especially from those who live here.

The markets which Thomas Gerard remarked upon in the seventeenth century were then long established, Taunton's the largest in the county at Domesday and held, of course, in the centre of town where the four principal roads still come together. Now its place has been taken by town-centre shops; the livestock market and its Saturday traders are some distance away, and the modern out-of-town shopping and leisure complex further away still, beyond the motorway. Today Taunton is regarded as a regional centre, at least in part because of its commercial strength and strategic position between Bristol and Exeter.

Taunton and its nearby towns are not, of course, what they once were. Thomas Gerard would probably be hard put to it to recognise them, though some of the surrounding villages appear not to have changed essentially for centuries. These photographs may help to suggest what has survived; at the same time each is an indicator of change, for every building in an ancient town is likely to be a replacement of something older, and what is there today may not be there tomorrow. Conversely, if Taunton's Farmers' Market is more than a short-term response to an agricultural crisis, buying and selling in the streets may return.

Taunton and Wellington will never again be centres of West-country cloth manufacture. Service industries and administration dominate, and Taunton has excellent communications by road and rail. Since the 1930s it has been home to county government; for much longer the home of county cricket. The county regiment had its headquarters here, its heroic days now recalled in memorials and fragile flags and some striking barrack buildings, mostly converted to residential uses of a more pacific kind. Here, too, are three public schools, with a fourth in Wellington, each with an international reputation. A website just discovered on the internet, however, by implication declares such attractions to be irrelevant: the town is for the young, who care little for heritage and more for restaurants, pubs and nightclubs. Entertainment value is what matters.

The towers of Taunton form, especially as seen from the railway, a memorable skyline. Reddish-purple Quantock stone and grey-white lias mark the colour range of the town's buildings. Apart from the churches of St Mary Magdalene and St James none is greatly distinguished but many, especially those in mellow brick, are elegant in a provincial way. Taunton boasts something from every century from the fourteenth to the present and a castle at its heart has parts a century earlier. Wellington, Wiveliscombe and their neighbours similarly offer to more mature visitors those snatches of heritage which are so rewarding.

Taunton Castle, once centre of the bishop of Winchester's estate, is heritage inside and out, and it has strong historical connections with many surrounding villages. Rents were paid in the Castle's exchequer room and complaints of lord and neighbour were heard if not answered in the court room. An echo of this feudal past is the court leet whose officers share among themselves the quaint titles of a past when butchers, leather dressers and corn chandlers shared unpaved streets with the public water supply and with bakers and alesellers who might attempt to cheat their customers on matters of weight or quality.

Away from the towns, Taunton's Vale, the Quantocks and the Levels offer differing landscapes whose village names recall owners of a distant past, like Cheddon and Staple Fitzpaine; their ancient tenure like West Buckland; their topography like Corfe or Heathfield. Hestercombe, a Quantock valley where some long-forgotten younger son settled, was a place known to Thomas Gerard as for long the chief seat of the Warre family. Over the last few years layers of history have been revealed beneath tangled undergrowth and indiscriminate commercial planting. Now from restored Classical temple arbour and Gothic alcove the Vale of Taunton and the town at its heart is revealed as a Warre descendant planned to reveal it.

Coplestone Warre Bampfylde, the creator of the landscape garden in the eighteenth century, fortunately recorded some of his creation in watercolours. The photographs here published will, in time, be of similar value as a record of a county town and its neighbours. But they are more than a record. Together they are a portrait, or rather a series of portraits; places and people in different seasons and different moods; glimpses of a way of life in a particular town and its hinterland which is home to many and temporary lodging for many more.

ROBERT DUNNING

IN THE TOWN

Looking down into the town centre, over the Market House.

The results of the recent enhancement of the town centre.

Old Market Centre – Taunton's modern
undercover shopping area opened in 1982.

One of the striking additions to Old Market Centre – The Taunton Toads!

Old Market Centre, site of the medieval pig market – only wooden pigs can now be seen.

Jarman's Court – named after Edward Jarman, a Taunton apothecary in business in the town in the eighteenth century.

Above County Walk,
a modern covered
shopping area.

Taunton's Cattle Market, still the town's agricultural centre.

Bath Place. A real gem at the heart of the town with a variety of small shops, including the renowned Women's Institute Market, and cottages. It was the main route west out of the town in the Middle Ages.

The Courtyard – a modern shopping precinct off St James' Street.

Riverside shopping.

High Street, a pedestrianised area popular for its shops, market and eating establishments. The street contains various interesting architectural details.

Old Municipal Buildings. The home of the borough government until 1987, it was built as a grammar school by Richard Fox, bishop of Winchester, in 1522.

The imposing entrance to
Old Municipal Buildings.

Shire Hall, built in 1855-58 to designs by W.B. Moffatt.

The Shire Hall is the current home of the Crown and County Courts.

Hammet Street, named after Sir Benjamin Hammet, a former Taunton MP, who was a prime mover in its creation in 1788.

Middle Street: eating versus exercise.

Market House. Completed in 1772 to a design by Coplestone Warre Bampfylde, it is pictured with the Burma war memorial in the foreground.

Fore Street, including Tudor Tavern. One of the oldest surviving buildings in the town with parts dating back to 1350 and now a favourite watering hole.

Taunton Castle. The castle dates from the thirteenth century and houses the Somerset County Museum. In 1685, 514 men who had followed the Duke of Monmouth were tried by Judge Jeffreys in the Great Hall.

Taunton Castle by floodlight.

Castle Bow, under the Castle Hotel.

The greenery-bedecked west front of the Castle Hotel.

The enduring fascination of Excalibur, on Castle Green.

The Winchester Arms.

Gray's Almshouses. Dating from 1635, these homes were founded
by Sir Robert Gray and include a small chapel which still retains its
original painted ceiling.

The St James' Street Almshouse, in the Castle grounds, rescued when a row of eight houses was demolished in 1897. Originally built about 1500, the house is furnished in the style of the early seventeenth century.

Huish Homes,
Magdalene Street.

More homes at St James'.

The Brewhouse. Taunton's premier centre for the visual and performing arts.

Tacchi-Morris arts centre, Heathfield School.

The Crescent. A fine series of Georgian
houses, now commercial offices.

Park Street. High Victorian gentility.

The Britannia Building Society. An imposing
Victorian feature in the town centre.

The Old Library. Former home to the town's library until 1996, it was built in 1905 with help from the Andrew Carnegie foundation. This is now another popular watering hole.

Mecca Bingo Hall. A grade II listed building, the Mecca Bingo Hall was opened in 1932 as the Gaumont Palace Cinema.

Heritage Trail Plaque. A brass plaque – one of many on Taunton's Heritage Trail, another way of seeing the town.

A detail of Safeways Supermarket, part of the changing face of Taunton, taken from the Riverside Walk.

County Hall – the headquarters of Somerset County Council since 1935 – designed by E. Vincent Harris.

Deane House, from which the Borough of Taunton is administered.

The Magistrates' Court, St John's Road.

Town Bridge. There has been a river crossing here since Saxon times. This bridge, built in 1895, replaced a medieval one, and is still adorned by the original lighting columns.

Two parts of the former School of Art.

Musgrove Park Hospital.

And where do you park? A worm's eye view of the multi-storey solution.

Gurds Shop Front. Originally built as a cottage, this menswear shop has been in the same family since the 1920s.

St Mary Magdalene. The tower
was completely rebuilt between
1858 and 1862.

Holy Trinity. A relatively modern church built to meet the demands of the growing town in 1842.

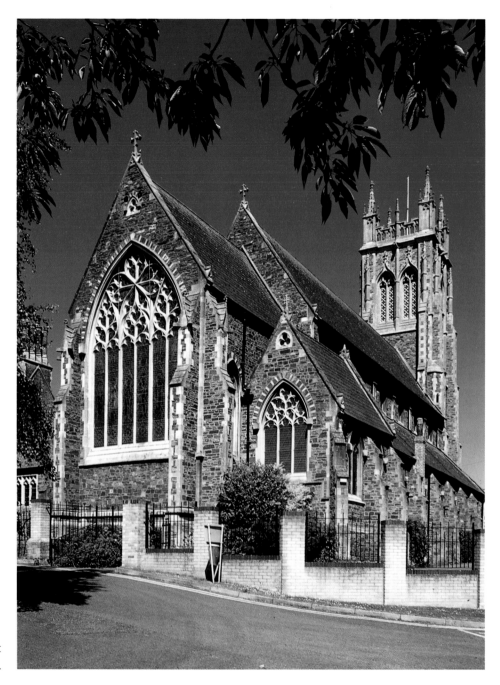

St George's Roman Catholic
church dates from 1861.

Unitarian Chapel former school rooms. A rich history of more than 300 years including Baptist and Presbyterian witness, noted for its fine galleried interior and two massive Corinthian pillars.

St John the Evangelist noted for its prominent spire.

Silver Street Baptist chapel built in 1814, its highly ornate Italian frontage added in 1870.

Taunton's new Library, Paul Street.

The source of all wisdom – the bustling Tourist Information Centre within the Library.

Dragon outside the Library. Created by Philip Thomason to celebrate the opening of the new Library in 1996. The dragon is an amalgamation of the crafts of pottery and stone carving.

Queen's College. Taunton's earliest public school, founded in 1843.

King's College. Founded by Canon Nathaniel Woodard in 1880.

Taunton School, with roots dating back to 1847.

Bishop Fox's School. On its new site off South Road.

SCAT. The buildings of the Somerset College of Arts and Technology.

Playtime at Bishop Henderson Primary School, Galmington.

OUT & ABOUT

Relaxing by the river – Goodland Gardens.

Vivary Park bandstand, dating from 1895, where every summer Sunday music can still be heard.

Fountain in Vivary Park, built in 1907 as a memorial to Queen Victoria. The Jellalabad Barracks on the left of the picture was part of the base of the County Regiment and was so named after the victory in Afghanistan in 1842.

Bowling in Vivary Park. 'Jack is King!'

Playtime in
Vivary Park.

Golf in Vivary Park. Fore!

On the level. Somerset versus Kent during
a Nat West Trophy match.

Cricket Ground – from on high. Somerset in action against World
Cup winners, Australia, in May 1999. Cricket has been played on this
riverside site since 1881. Fans of the game will be familiar with this
superb site, the twin church towers and the backdrop of the
Quantock Hills.

Medieval Barn. Current home of the Somerset Cricket Museum, this medieval building was a gatehouse of the Augustinian Priory and was later used as a barn.

At the races. Taunton Racecourse has been a National Hunt course since 1927.

Taunton Agricultural Show. Each summer this popular show indicates the importance of the farming industry to the area.

Water Festival. Taunton's Water Festival, French Weir, August 1997.

Flower Show. The Chelsea of the West –
Taunton's premier annual flower show.

The foothills of Quantocks from the town. St James' church on the left, St Mary Magdalene on the right.

View over the Vale From Corfe Hill.

The Vale as seen from West
Bagborough in the Quantocks.

Lydeard Hill, looking
towards Taunton.

Down in the Vale: Trull.

West Somerset Railway. At 20 miles, this is the UK's longest privately-owned steam railway line, restored after closure in 1971.

Bishops Lydeard Station, start of the 20-mile journey to Minehead.

The Levels. West Sedgemoor, part of the Somerset Levels, one of the most important wetland areas in the country.

Products of the Levels: basket maker at Meare Green.

Hestercombe House. The headquarters of the Somerset Fire Service, the house is a Victorian Italianate villa.

Hestercombe Garden. A popular tourist attraction considered to be one of the finest examples of the partnership between Sir Edward Lutyens and Gertrude Jekyll.

In the formal garden at Hestercombe: the Plat.

The Pergola at
Hestercombe.

The Secret Landscape Gardens at
Hestercombe, created by Coplestone Warre
Bampfylde between 1750 and 1786.

Hestercombe: the Waterfall.

Cothelstone, Manor and church.

Hatch Court. Originating in the seventeenth century, a Bath stone mansion in the Palladian style.

Poundisford Park, Pitminster, a sixteenth-century merchant's mansion.

Cothay Manor, Kittisford.

Stoke St Gregory church.

Cheddon Fitzpaine church.

Fivehead, cross.

Corfe church.

Trull church.

Heatherton Grange gatehouse, Bradford-on-Tone.

Fyne Court, current home of the Somerset Wildlife Trust.

Sandhill Park.

The former Tone Vale Hospital.

Tone Vale is the oldest building within the new village of Cotford St Luke.

Wiveliscombe – an historic market town situated on the edge of the Brendon Hills.

Milverton. North Street, in the picturesque village which has been designated as a Heritage Settlement, in the Vale of Taunton Deane.

Blagdon Hill, in the parish of Pitminster.

Tonedale, Wellington. Fox Brothers' former factory.

A Noble Comb machine used in their cloth manufacturing process.

Wellington, former
Town Hall.

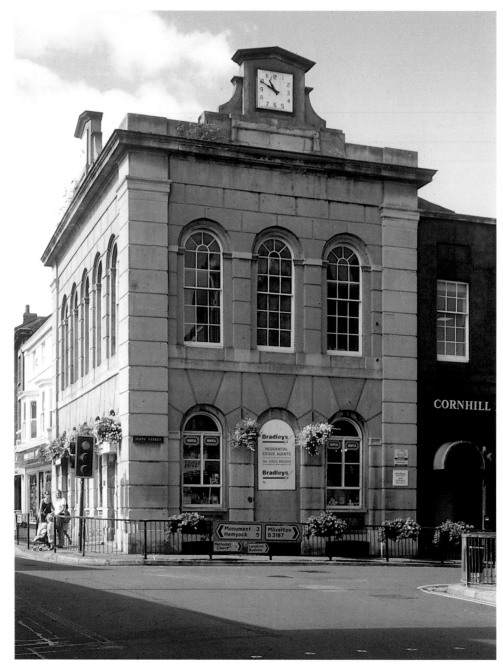

North Curry, Church Road.

North Curry is also known for its fine church, dubbed the 'Cathedral of the Moors'.

Halse, village centre.

Bishop's Hull church.

Blackdowns. Otterhead Lakes, owned by the local water company, are a well known recreation area.

Maunsel Lock. The Bridgwater-Taunton Canal, dating from the early nineteenth century, still in use today, and popular for boating, fishing, walking and cycling.

Cycling on the Quantocks. The first Area of Outstanding Natural Beauty designated in England.

Sheppy's Cider Museum. Sheppy's have been making cider in the Westcountry for some eighty years.

Bradford-on-Tone.

Kingston St Mary.

Stoke St Mary.

Rumwell, Bishop's Hull.

Blackbrook Inn, Ruishton.

Staple Fitzpaine.

PLUTO

This tiny planet welcomes you
to the Somerset Space Walk. The real
Pluto is 2200 kms acros, from here to
Istanbul! The scale of the space walk -
530,000,000/1 - reduces the real Pluto to the
tiny metal sphere that you see above!
However, do not expect to find the model
Sun around the corner - no, that is 11.3 kms
away at Maunsel Lock. On your way you
will walk through the Solar System,
discovering the other planets
in their places.

BRIDGWATER 22.5KMS

THE SOMERSET SPACE WALK

Space Walk: Pluto. One of the planets on the Somerset Space Walk – a true scale model of our solar system placed along the towpath of the Taunton-Bridgwater Canal.

The Sun at Maunsel, the centre of the Space Walk.

Wellington Monument. A landmark for miles around, the 175 ft column was erected in honour of the Duke of Wellington.

Burton Pynsent Monument. Set up by William Pitt the elder as a tribute to his benefactor Sir William Pynsent.

The Athelney
Memorial, erected
in 1801 by John
Slade of Maunsel to
mark the site of
Athelney Abbey.

Burrow Mump: a natural conical hill topped
with the unfinished eighteenth-century
St Michael's chapel.

Obridge Viaduct.

Apples galore!

A Taunton byway.

Caring for the roads: an end and a beginning.